remember

WORLD WAR II

remember

WORLD WAR II

Kids Who Survived
Tell Their Stories

Dorinda Makanaõnalani Nicholson
with a foreword by **Madeleine K. Albright**

NATIONAL
GEOGRAPHIC

WASHINGTON, D.C.

For—
THE EUROPE KIDS: Fred, Hedi, Jirina, Lilly, Olga, and Solange
THE PACIFIC KIDS: Eiko, Joy, Judy, and Thompson
THE HOME FRONT KIDS: Allan, Betty Jo, Dora Mae, and James
Now, new generations of kids will know what it is like to be a child of war.

STAFF FOR THIS BOOK
Suzanne Patrick Fonda, *Project Editor*
Bea Jackson, *Art Director*
David M. Seager, *Designer*
Callie Broaddus, *Associate Designer*
Lori Epstein, *Senior Photo Editor*
Janet A. Dustin, *Illustrations Coordinator*
Carl Mehler, *Director of Maps*
Matt Chwastyk and Nicholas P. Rosenbach, *Map Research and Production*
Paige Towler, *Editorial Assistant*
R. Gary Colbert, *Production Director*
Lewis R. Bassford, *Production Manager*
Jennifer Hoff, *Manager, Production Services*

PUBLISHED BY THE NATIONAL GEOGRAPHIC SOCIETY
Gary E. Knell, *President and CEO*
John M. Fahey, *Chairman of the Board*
Melina Gerosa Bellows, *Chief Education Officer*
Declan Moore, *Chief Media Officer*
Hector Sierra, *Senior Vice President and General Manager, Book Division*

SENIOR MANAGEMENT TEAM, KIDS PUBLISHING AND MEDIA
Nancy Laties Feresten, *Senior Vice President;* Jennifer Emmett, *Vice
President, Editorial Director, Kids Books;* Julie Vosburgh Agnone, *Vice
President, Editorial Operations;* Rachel Buchholz, *Editor and Vice Presi-
dent,* NG Kids *magazine;* Michelle Sullivan, *Vice President, Kids Digital;*
Eva Absher-Schantz, *Design Director;* Jay Sumner, *Photo Director;* Hannah
August, *Marketing Director;* R. Gary Colbert, *Production Director*

DIGITAL
Anne McCormack, *Director;* Laura Goertzel, Sara Zeglin, *Producers;* Jed
Winer, *Special Projects Assistant;* Emma Rigney, *Creative Producer;* Brian
Ford, *Video Producer;* Bianca Bowman, *Assistant Producer;* Natalie Jones,
Senior Product Manager

Text is set in ITC New Baskerville.
Survivor accounts are set in Univers 57 Condensed.

The National Geographic Society is one of the world's largest nonprofit
scientific and educational organizations. Founded in 1888 to "increase and
diffuse geographic knowledge," the Society's mission is to inspire people
to care about the planet. It reaches more than 400 million people worldwide
each month through its official journal, *National Geographic,* and other
magazines; National Geographic Channel; television documentaries; music;
radio; films; books; DVDs; maps; exhibitions; live events; school publishing
programs; interactive media; and merchandise. National Geographic has
funded more than 10,000 scientific research, conservation, and exploration
projects and supports an education program promoting geographic literacy.

For more information, please visit nationalgeographic.com,
call 1-800-NGS LINE (647-5463), or write to the following address:

NATIONAL GEOGRAPHIC SOCIETY
1145 17th Street N.W.
Washington, D.C. 20036-4688 U.S.A.

Visit us online at nationalgeographic.com/books

For librarians and teachers: ngchildrensbooks.org

More for kids from National Geographic: kids.nationalgeographic.com

For information about special discounts for bulk purchases, please contact
National Geographic Books Special Sales: ngspecsales@ngs.org

**National Geographic supports K–12 educators with ELA Common Core
Resources. Visit natgeoed.org/commoncore for more information.**

Printed in Hong Kong
15/THK/1

ACKNOWLEDGMENTS
Grateful appreciation to Denise, Hazel, Marie Claire, Nera, Peter,
and Tetsu for also sharing their World War II stories. To my husband,
Larry, for his artistry, research, and critical eye in seeking the vivid
historical images that illustrate this book. A very special thanks
to former Secretary of State Madeleine Albright and her staff for
providing such an appropriate and insightful foreword. Finally, to
Suzanne Patrick Fonda for sharing the vision, guiding the way, and
for being my very first editor.

Library of Congress Cataloging-in-Publication Data
available on request

2015 paperback edition ISBN: 978-1-4263-2251-8
2015 reinforced library edition ISBN: 978-1-4263-2356-0

PHOTO CREDITS
NA = National Archives; NGS = National Geographic Society;
NHC = U.S. Naval Historical Center, USHMM = U.S. Holocaust
Museum, OWI = Office of War Information

Front Cover, NA; 4–5, NA; 7 (top), Corbis; 7 (center), Patricia
O'Meara Robbins from *Hawaii Goes to War;* 7 (bottom), courtesy
Honolulu Star-Bulletin; 8, courtesy Madeleine K. Albright; 10,
Corbis; 11, courtesy Olga Held Bruner; 12, USHMM; 13 (left), Wiener
Library; 13 (right), USHMM; 14 (both), courtesy Hedi Wachenheimer
Epstein; 15 (top), USHMM; 15 (bottom), courtesy Jirina Zizkovska
Levine; 16, courtesy Fred Losch; 17 (left), Corbis; 17 (right), author's
collection; 19 (both), courtesy Solange Berger Chomon; 20 (top), NA;
20 (bottom), Therese Bonney University of California at Berkeley; 23,
24 (top, both), courtesy Hedi Wachenheimer Epstein; 24 (bottom),
courtesy Libu "Lilly" Lebovitz Segelstein; 25, USHMM; 26, courtesy
Bill Moore collection; 27, courtesy D-Day Museum; 29, Corbis; 30,
Patricia O'Meara Robbins from *Hawaii Goes to War;* 31, courtesy
Thompson Izawa; 33, courtesy Judy Rhoades Davis; 34, NA; 35, NHC;
36 (top), Patricia O'Meara Robbins; 36 (bottom), War Depository
Collection University of Hawaii; 37, courtesy John Bowles; 38 (both),
courtesy Joy Crichton Preston; 39, Getty; 40, courtesy Joy Crichton
Preston; 41, courtesy Eiko Arai Moyer; 42, Mainichi Newspaper,
Tokyo; 44, courtesy *Honolulu Star-Bulletin;* 45, courtesy James J.
Fisher; 46 (both), courtesy Allan Hida; 47, 48, NA; 48–49, courtesy
Allan Hida; 50, courtesy Dora Mae Boone Traul; 51, OWI; 52 (top),
courtesy Betty Jo Oetting Morris; 52 (bottom), courtesy the author;
53, courtesy Chicago Park School District; 54–55, Corbis; 58 (top),
Therese Bonney University of California at Berkeley; 58 (center), NA;
58 (bottom), courtesy the author; 60, NA.

COVER: *Two children watch from a pile of rubble as American
troops leave the liberated but bombed-out city of St.-Lo, France.*

TITLE PAGE: *A nighttime air raid by the German Luftwaffe leaves
three British children homeless.*

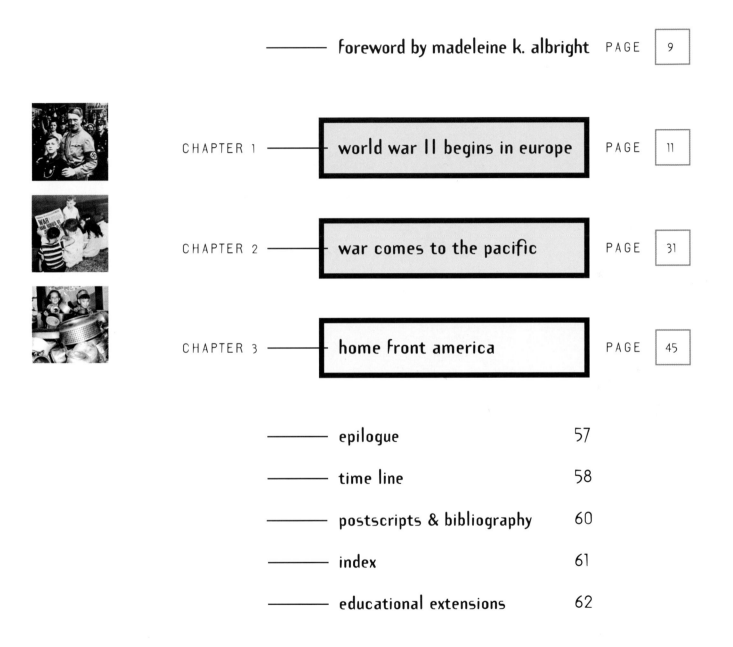

Madeleine Albright (center) at the early stages of the war, standing with her two grandmothers, Růžena Spieglová and Olga Körbelová. She later learned that they had died during the war.

Foreword

To a child growing up in a time of war, the abnormal is the only reality one has experienced. This is what life is like: to spend your evenings in a bomb shelter; to fear thunder in the sky; to move about from place to place; to watch adults for signs of reassurance or warning; to listen for clues to what is really going on; to have loved ones disappear; to be told you are brave when you are only bewildered; to hope for a return to the real normalcy you have never known.

I was lucky. Born in Czechoslovakia in 1937, I escaped with my parents after Hitler invaded my homeland the following year. We went first to Yugoslavia and then to England, where I spent the war, living in a succession of homes. There I learned a new language and to eat new kinds of foods. Lunch each day was a serving of cold meat and something called bubble and squeak, a mixture of leftover potatoes and cabbage that took its name from the sound it made in your stomach after you ate it.

My father worked for the Czechoslovak government in exile, doing broadcasts over the British radio network. He was also an air raid warden. We acquired a large steel table that was advertised as able to save a family hiding under it when a house was bombed. The table became the centerpiece of our daily routine. We ate on it, played around and on top of it, and when the sirens sounded pulled down the blackout shades and slept under it.

After the noon meal on Sundays, my father walked up and down our small garden in the company of friends. They paced with their hands clasped behind their backs as European men do, my father always with a pipe and a puff of smoke wreathing his head. It wasn't until much later that I understood what they had been discussing — the progress of the war and the prospects for returning home.

I was eight when that glorious day finally arrived. I was scared out of my wits, flying to Czechoslovakia in the belly of a bomber. Unlike some European capitals, Prague had not been bombed. Physically, it was a beautiful, magical place. But the country had suffered terribly from eight years of demoralizing occupation, economic catastrophe, and the destruction of much of its Jewish population. It was not until I became U.S. secretary of state in 1997 that I learned through a reporter's research that my own family heritage was Jewish, and that three of my grandparents and numerous other family members had perished in Nazi death camps.

"War is hell," said U.S. Army General William Tecumseh Sherman. Whether war is especially cruel to children depends on the particular case. Sometimes it is easier when we are young and do not fully understand. Sometimes it is harder because the young cannot protect themselves. Either way, war is tragic. Although war destroys, like any part of life, it also teaches. Together let us search for lessons in the experiences recounted and the images reproduced in this warm and compelling book.

Madeleine Albright

Hitler was a brilliant speaker. Speaking slowly, quietly at first, he prescribed simple cures for Germany's problems while gradually raising the emotional intensity to a full fury. With calculated gestures he awed his listeners into adoring submission. He was the most dangerous man in Europe.

CHAPTER 1

world war II begins in europe

The origins of World War II are rooted within World War I, known as the "war to end all wars." The terms of the Versailles Treaty, which ended the war, angered Germany. She was bitter. Her pride was hurt.

When Hitler came to power in 1933, Germany was poor, food was scarce, and Germans had lost hope. Hitler's impassioned, screeching voice had the power to fire up a crowd's emotions. Thousands cheered when he promised to regain territory taken by the war, provide jobs, and supply plenty to eat. Believing his promises, Germans began to regain lost pride and to hope again.

Driven by the belief the German "race" was superior, he persuaded his followers to eliminate most religions and anyone who was "imperfect": homosexuals, Gypsies, the disabled, union leaders, anyone who opposed him, and his main target: all Jews.

Hitler chose Nuremberg for a massive Nazi pep rally and parade to excite Germans to prepare for war.

OLGA HELD, August 1933, Nuremberg, Germany ————— Olga Held and her father walked hand in hand from their home in Nuremberg to a rally and parade for Hitler's Nazi Party. Swastika flags filled every window. The city swarmed with uniformed men: the S.S. (Schutzstaffel, or Secret Service), who wore black, and the S.A. (storm troopers) in brown.

Olga remembers, "As we passed them they said, 'Heil Hitler' accompanied by a stiff-arm salute. When we arrived at the parade grounds, my right arm ached from all the saluting.

"I squeezed past the legs of adults to join children in the front row. From a distance an open black limousine advanced slowly. As it neared, I saw Hitler's face, his black mustache, piercing blue eyes, and thin smile. He stood behind the windshield of the car, his right arm rigid in a salute to the thousands hailing him.

Olga Held on her sixth birthday

11

"Right in front of me, the car stopped. Hitler stepped out, walked briskly along the line of spectators, and shook the outstretched hands of all the children, including me. Then he turned around and stepped back into the car.

"Thrilled, I ran to my father. I tugged his shirt-sleeve to get his attention and boasted, 'Our führer shook hands with me.' Father just looked down at me and didn't say one word."

An idolizing crowd greets the führer with the Heil Hitler (Long live Hitler) salute. Hitler believed his followers were part of a superior master race called Aryans. He blamed the Jews for all of Germany's problems.

To avenge Nazi mistreatment of his parents, Herschel Grynszpan (above) was arrested for killing a German diplomat. Hitler used the killing as an excuse to punish all Jews by ordering synagogues and Jewish shops (left) destroyed. November 9, 1938, became known as *Kristallnacht,* "the night of broken glass."

For the next five years, Germany dramatically expanded its armed forces. On March 12, 1938, Hitler began his conquest of Europe with the annexation of Austria. No one stopped him. In a few months, he took all of Czechoslovakia.

On November 7, 1938, a teenage Jew of Polish heritage shot and killed a German official to avenge Nazi mistreatment of his parents. His parents, along with all other Polish Jews, had been forced out of Germany and deported back to Poland. After the shooting event, Hitler had an excuse to punish all Jews in Germany. Two days later, Jewish shops and synagogues were destroyed. Homes were looted or burned in the countrywide attack. Broken glass was so plentiful following the destruction that the November 9 rampage was called *Kristallnacht,* "crystal night," or "night of broken glass." The life of every Jew in Europe was in jeopardy.

Hedi Wachenheimer with grandmother Lina

Hedi wore this tag on the Kindertransport to England.

HEDI WACHENHEIMER, November 1938, Kippenheim, Germany

It was a sunny but cold day in Kippenheim, Germany. Fourteen-year-old Hedi Wachenheimer listened as the school principal spoke to her class. She remembers, "He then pointed his finger at me and said, 'Get out you dirty Jew.' I could not believe this formerly kind, gentle person would say this to me. He repeated it, took me by the elbow, and shoved me out of the classroom. I wondered what I had done. Before I could answer my question, the children came out of the classroom. Some pushed me, others called me a dirty Jew.

"When I got home, I noticed the green shutters were closed. They were never closed during the day. The door was locked, and no one answered the door bell. Walking toward me was the village's meanest Nazi. I was afraid to talk to him, but I wanted to find my mother. 'I don't know where the g— damn bitch is, but if I find her, I'll kill her,' was his answer. I took off as fast as I could to my aunt's house.

"My mother opened the door. She said about ten minutes after I left for school, Nazis came to the house and arrested my father, taking him away in his pajamas. They did not allow him to dress or to wear a coat even though it was cold. A couple of Nazis stayed behind and broke all the windows, some furniture, and dishes. After they left, mother closed the shutters, locked the house, and while still wearing her nightgown, ran to my aunt's house. She later learned that all Jewish men and boys 16 and older were taken.

"Shortly after I arrived there, a human chain of men and boys, shackled together four in a row and shoved along by the S.S., marched past my aunt's house. In this group were my father, uncle, and other males I knew. My mother practically hung me out of the second story window calling to my father, 'We have Hedi, we're together.' Whether he heard or saw me, we don't know. We watched the group until they trudged around the bend in the road and out of sight.

"I was so traumatized by these events, I did not let my mother or my aunt out of my sight. If one had to go to the bathroom, I insisted all three of us go together. We moved in an extra bed to allow the three of us to sleep in the same room.

"Jewish children could not attend school, Jewish businesses were closed, Jewish doctors or lawyers could not practice, Jews could not go to hospitals or be treated by a Christian doctor. Most synagogues [Jewish places of worship] in Germany and Austria were burned to the ground.

Jewish refugee children, members of the first Kindertransport en route to Harwich, England. Between December 1938 and September 1939, almost 10,000 unaccompanied refugee children escaped to Great Britain, where they were housed in foster homes or hostels.

"On May 18, 1939, I was able to leave Germany on a Kindertransport to England. There were almost 10,000 children transported in the nine months before the war began. I was child #5580. I hoped to be apart from my mother and father for only a short time, but I never saw them again."

Jews weren't Hitler's only targets. Anyone who spoke out against him or his Nazi Party was at risk. Most of Europe lived in fear.

JIRINA ZIZKOVSKA, March 1939, Plzen, Czechoslovakia

Jirina Zizkovska at church, 1942

Fifteen-year-old Jirina Zizkovska lived near Plzen, in southwest Czechoslovakia. Jirina was the youngest child in her family. Her parents were angry and terrified when Hitler was given part of their country.

"We knew the Nazis were coming. Soon the troops would reach our small village of 3,000 people. Many of our neighbors, mostly Jewish, had already fled," says Jirina.

"My chore was to sweep the sidewalk in front of our three-story-apartment building before breakfast. I remember it was cold that March 15th morning. I opened the door to the street and began to sweep. The straw broom scratched across the stone walkway as I busied myself. I heard them long before I saw them. The marching—the pounding of hundreds of boots—that meant hundreds of soldiers. Running up the stairs, I screamed, 'Mother, they're here. The Nazis are here!'"

While Hitler continued his conquests, he demanded his homeland followers obey him without question, especially the youth. Schoolchildren were instructed how to salute with their right arm and say "Heil Hitler!" Girls, age 10 through 14, were taught physical fitness and homemaking skills. Boys at age 10 joined the Jungvolk (Hitler Youth) to develop skills of war. All children were "programmed" to build a superior German race.

Fred Losch, in the third grade

FRED LOSCH, September 1939, Lötzen, East Prussia, Germany

Fred Losch of East Prussia, Germany, joined the Jungvolk in 1937 when he was ten years old.

"I remember the first hike. It began on a Saturday afternoon. We had to walk 15 kilometers [about 10 miles] with our backpack, called 'affe' (monkey) because it had a hairy back cover. It was so demanding, I lost all the food I had eaten that day. When a visiting ranking officer spoke to us, he lauded our effort and gave us permission to wear the scout knife and the shoulder belt, status symbols of the Jungvolk.

"My last trip with the Jungvolk was a bike trip. We were on the road to Tannenberg for three days. On August 27, 1939, we got word to return home immediately. The roads were increasingly crowded with military vehicles—it was clear something was up. We got home, and a few days later, the war began. It was September 1, 1939."

On that day, one million German soldiers marched into Poland. It was a hopeless contest for the Poles, who had only horses and swords to fight German planes and tanks. The invasion of Poland introduced Hitler's attack technique called "blitzkrieg" (lightning war), combining speed and surprise.

Powerful Stuka dive-bombers attacked first by bombing airfields and providing air

The führer's ideal youth were "slim and slender, swift as greyhounds, tough as leather, and hard as Krupp steel." By 1939, there were eight million Hitler Youth. Nazi mothers were awarded medals for producing large families. The one shown here is for bearing six to seven children.

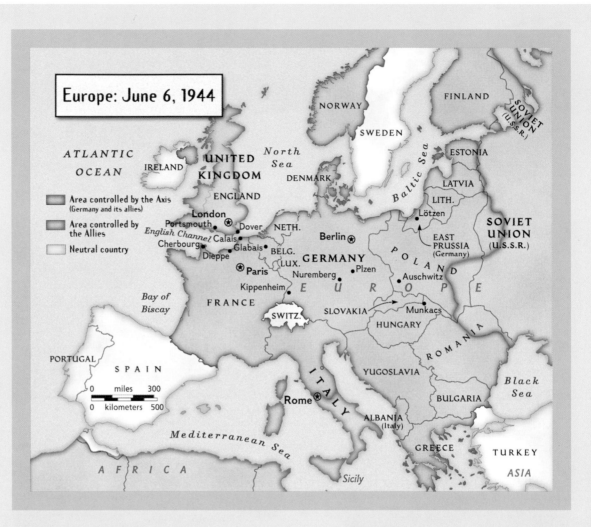

Europe: June 6, 1944

ATLANTIC OCEAN

Area controlled by the Axis (Germany and its allies)

Area controlled by the Allies

Neutral country

IRELAND

UNITED KINGDOM

ENGLAND

London

Portsmouth

English Channel

Cherbourg

Dieppe

Calais

Glabais

Dover

NETH.

BELG.

LUX.

Paris

Kippenheim

Nuremberg

Plzen

GERMANY

Berlin

POLAND

EAST PRUSSIA (Germany)

Auschwitz

SOVIET UNION (U.S.S.R.)

Lötzen

Munkacs

Bay of Biscay

FRANCE

SWITZ.

SLOVAKIA

HUNGARY

ROMANIA

PORTUGAL

SPAIN

0 miles 300

0 kilometers 500

Rome

ITALY

ALBANIA (Italy)

YUGOSLAVIA

BULGARIA

GREECE

Black Sea

TURKEY

ASIA

Mediterranean Sea

Sicily

AFRICA

North Sea

DENMARK

SWEDEN

NORWAY

FINLAND

SOVIET UNION (U.S.S.R.)

ESTONIA

LATVIA

LITH.

Baltic Sea

EUROPE

Hitler believed he was meant to rule the world: "Today, Europe, tomorrow, the world." This map shows how much of Europe Germany had acquired by June 6, 1944, the date of the Allied invasion of the continent. Hitler wanted more, especially the United Kingdom and the Soviet Union.

cover for tanks. By surging ahead deep behind enemy lines, the tanks divided troops into separate pockets and cut them off from supplies. Then slower-moving conventional artillery and infantry moved in to crush the isolated troops for an easy victory. The Stuka bomber combined with the "blitzkrieg" technique spread fear and death as Hitler advanced across Europe.

No countries tried to stop him. France and England declared war but didn't attack. Hitler used this "Phony War" time to strengthen his fortifications along the French border and plan his next conquests.

On April 9, 1940, Hitler attacked Denmark and Norway, again using the swift "blitzkrieg." Denmark fell that same day; Norway fell a few months later. The rest of Europe waited for the dictator's next move. A month later his troops marched into the Netherlands, Belgium, and Luxembourg.

Before Hitler's army began its march toward Belgium, five-year-old Solange Berger, her eight-year-old sister, and her parents prepared to flee with the 153 people of their small village near Waterloo. Before leaving, Solange's father dug a big hole in their garden. Into the hole went the family valuables, and Solange's cherished doll. "I told father to put her in extra deep so she would be safe, and to cover her carefully.

Solange Berger at her first communion

"Everyone went on the road," recalls Solange, "with just a few things. Some had horses, we had two bicycles. I rode on the back of my sister's bicycle. Everyone just followed, one behind the other. No one wanted to be left alone, so we went as a village. But in two days, we all got separated in the long column of families, and nobody knew anyone. At night we slept in farms with nothing to eat. When we asked for food or water, people wanted to be paid.

"We crossed over into France and hoped we could find a safe place, but the German Army was already there. So, why stay? We turned around and walked the 150 kilometers [about 90 miles] back to our small village. We saw bombed bridges as we got closer to home. It was terrible to see. When we got home, the German Army had occupied our village, and we found two Nazi officers living in our house."

Solange and her sister were terrified of the German officers. "I still remember the crisp sound of their cleated boots across our wood floors. At night my sister and I would pull the covers up tight around us, completely covering ourselves. Then it seemed safe to sneak a peek as their boots clicked out of the room.

Solange's cherished doll survived the war.

"Our King surrendered Belgium to the Germans almost immediately. We had to share our home with the Nazi officers for the remainder of the war."

Belgium's surrender was a death threat to France and England. With Belgium's collapse, the Germans smashed remaining defense lines and sent a Panzer tank convoy racing toward the English Channel. The retreating British and French troops were trapped at the French seaport of Dunkirk. A call went out for any kind of boat to evacuate the soldiers from certain destruction: tiny fishing vessels, sightseeing boats, even barges. The Luftwaffe (Germany's Air Force) strafed and bombed the trapped men as they dropped their equipment and clambered on board the unarmed boats to escape to England.

A Frenchman weeps in the midst of his solemn countrymen as German soldiers occupy France. While the Nazi flag flew over France, some French people surrendered, some sided with Hitler, some stayed neutral, and some became underground Resistance fighters.

War demands constant supplies of ammunition and weapons. The Nazis forced the handicapped, prisoners of war, and mostly those too young or too old to fight to work as slave labor in weapons and munitions factories.

The heroic rescue of 330,000 troops was a huge boost to the morale of the British.

With the British gone, the French Army fell apart and retreated. Masses of French civilians fled from the German troops as they marched toward Paris. Roads were jammed with cars, carts, bicycles, baby carriages—anything that would move.

French citizens wept openly as German troops marched into their capital city. The Nazis set up elaborate headquarters in luxurious buildings. On June 14, 1940, the Nazi flag flew over the Champs Elysées, the most beautiful boulevard in Paris. Three days later, France surrendered. Some of France stayed neutral with business as usual in Paris. The part of the country that supported Hitler was called Vichy. People opposed to Hitler formed a network of underground Resistance fighters.

Meanwhile in Germany, most young men were called into the armed forces. This created a labor shortage at farms and factories. The manpower shortage was filled by the handicapped or those too old to fight, by prisoners of war, or by those too young to go to war, including Olga Held, who was now 14.

OLGA — "In July, 1940, I was on a train with seven other girls to pick hops [grain used for making beer for the soldiers]," Olga recalls. "None of us had ever seen a hops farm. No one mentioned that we were forced to do this. When the train halted, I saw miles and miles of poles sticking straight up from the ground, each covered with a green vine.

"A farmer came for us with his wagon, and told us that we would work from 6 a.m. to 6 p.m. and sleep on the straw in his barn for the next three weeks. We were expected to pick five full bushels each day, and were to be paid the equivalent of 50 cents per bushel.

"In ten days, my hands were as black as the hands of a chimney sweep. I washed and washed them, but the shameful color would not disappear. The farmer's wife chuckled at my efforts, and told me that the black color would wear off in a few weeks, but it took five months. By the 21st day, I had picked 84 bushels."

By 1940, Germany ruled most of Europe. Great Britain was Hitler's next target. He ordered deadly submarines, called U-boats, to sink any supply ships headed to Britain. The U-boats were so successful that starvation and defeat were a real possibility for Britain.

To invade Britain, Hitler would do what had worked before—begin with an air attack to weaken ground targets and rule supreme over the skies. On July 10, 1940, the Luftwaffe bombed British ships in the English Channel. The Battle of Britain had begun. It would be mostly an air war, the first air war in history. Britain's RAF, the Royal Air Force, was outnumbered, but they had a new weapon—radar. This new electronic device enabled the RAF to detect and track the Luftwaffe from miles away, even at night. Although the air attacks continued, the determination and resistance of the RAF, along with the radar, saved Britain from invasion.

HEDI ——— Fifteen-year-old Hedi Wachenheimer was now living in London with a foster family. Although she was safely out of Germany, she was sad and lonely. She missed her parents and rural life in Kippenheim. Britain was often rainy and foggy, she knew little English, and the food was very different. She longed for her mother's arms instead of the arms of strangers. Blackouts became a way of life. Every night, as soon as it was dark, air raid wardens went from house to house to be sure not one sliver of light was visible. The wail of a siren meant enemy bombers were nearby.

"I slept fully dressed, with a packed suitcase ready to go to the basement when the bombing sounded close by. Once I went to a bomb shelter in the nearby park when there was an unexploded land mine in the next block. There was a time when the bombing was so prolonged and intense that I spent a couple of nights on the subway platform, sleep interrupted as trains came in and out of the station."

Back in Hedi's village of Kippenheim, all Jews were forced from their homes into drab army trucks with German soldiers standing guard. Non-Jews watched while the Jews, single suitcase clutched in hand, disappeared into the trucks, never to be seen again. Among them were Hedi's parents, deported on October 22, 1940, to Camp de Gurs, in Vichy, France.

After failing to conquer Britain, Hitler turned traitor on his ally Joseph Stalin, dictator of Russia. On June 22, 1941, three million German troops positioned themselves along the Russian border. Hitler, who was sure Russia would surrender in six weeks, was astonished by the fierce resistance of all Russians, not just the soldiers. He also didn't reckon with Russia's mightiest weapon, its severe winters. Expecting the

This deportation photo was taken secretly in Hedi's village on October 22, 1940. Her family, along with all the other Jews in her village, were loaded into trucks guarded by Nazi soldiers as non-Jews watched. Jews all over Europe disappeared into trucks and were never seen again.

Last postcard to Hedi from her mother. She tells Hedi, "It will be a long time till you hear from me again, keep your head high." There was no return address.

battle to be a short one, German troops did not come with winter clothing. Tanks bogged down in icy mud, and their engines froze solid. Thousands of German soldiers froze to death. The German Army finally surrendered in February 1943. The blitzkrieg style of warfare suffered its first major defeat.

Meanwhile, Hitler had declared war on the United States in December 1941, and on January 20, 1942, the Wannsee Conference was held in Berlin to determine "The Final Solution of the Jewish Question." Hitler's troops built camps to kill Jews or to work them to death. The Holocaust, the name by which this extermination became known, resulted in the slaughter of six million Jews.

HEDI

The Red Cross delivered messages between Hedi Wachenheimer in England and her imprisoned parents. She remembers, "In their last message, my father's in August, and my mother's in September, both parents wrote they were being deported to an unknown destination and it would be a long time before I would hear from them again. In my mother's postcard, dated September 4, 1942, she wrote she was traveling to the East. She is saying a final good-bye to me. There was no return address. She urged me to be brave, hold my head up high, never lose my courage, and to remember my parents. I later learned both my parents were deported to Auschwitz, the death camp. I never heard from them again."

Lilly, photographed in a displaced persons camp after the war

LIBU (LILLY) LEBOVITZ, March 1943, Munkacs, Czechoslovakia

Before the Jews were deported to the camps, they were forced into one section of town. This confined area was called the ghetto. "It was only about a mile from my home. I didn't understand why we had to live in a big barracks-like building and couldn't go home. There was just open space on bare floors to sleep," recalls then 14-year-old Libu ("Lilly") Lebovitz. Her family lived in the Carpathian Mountains of Czechoslovakia. "Our ghetto provided the workers for a Nazi brick factory. Every day a bunch of our people disappeared into trucks and didn't return. Then it was our family's turn. The truck took us to the trains."

Lilly and her family were jammed into cattle cars overfilled with men, women, and children headed for Auschwitz. The cars had no windows or other openings. More than 150 bodies

Child survivors of Auschwitz, wearing adult-size prisoner jackets, stand behind a barbed wire fence. The children on the right wearing knitted hats are twins. These twins were used for medical experiments three times a week for six to eight hours at a time.

crisscrossed on top of each other. The lucky ones on top of the human pile got the most air. They also escaped the human waste that sifted down through each layer as the train swayed along the tracks.

"We arrived at Auschwitz at night. The doors opened, and the deafening noise—dogs barking, and you can't even hear yourself, and the guards kept yelling at us, 'Arous' ['get out'].

"The guards shoved my mother and my baby sister off to one side. They were killed right away in the gas chambers. My older brother and my father survived for a while.

"My sister Lea and I were marched with others into a big barracks and told to undress completely. They shaved you, everywhere, even your head. All of us began to cry. I couldn't find my sister Lea.

"When she came out, I didn't recognize her. I kept calling, 'Lea, Lea.' You know, you are all naked, and your hair is all cut off. It's a sight you've never experienced, never expected. In the next room they gave you one striped dress.

"Lea and I lived in 'C' Camp with 30,000 other young females. We had cots, two-tier, shared by five girls. If one needed to turn, we all had to turn at once. For food, there was one pot of soup, usually split-pea with no spoon, for each meal. We would each take five sips from the pot then pass it on, the next person would take five sips. If there was any left, we passed it around again. At night we got a piece of bread.

"From the 30,000 in 'C' camp, we heard only 200 would be selected to work in a slave labor camp. My sister and I pinched our faces to look healthy. Others in camp tried to get beet juice to color their cheeks. My sister and I were picked. That meant we could leave certain death at Auschwitz and become slave labor at Reichenbach, a camp to produce ammunition for the Nazi Army.

"At Reichenbach, Lea and I walked five kilometers [3.5 miles] in wooden shoes to go to work. In the bitter winter we wrapped rags around our feet. It was very cold with lots of snow. If you fell down, the guards took care of you quickly.

"A German foreman took pity on my sister and me because we were so young, just 14 and 15. He would bring some extra bread and leave it on the table for us. My sister would worry about me even though she was younger. She claimed she wasn't hungry and gave her bread to me."

European radio

For families living under Nazi rule who were fortunate enough to have a radio, news broadcasts from England on the BBC (British Broadcasting Corporation) were a lifeline of hope. However, listening to any foreign broadcasts was illegal. In 1943, it became punishable by death. Olga Held and her family risked that punishment every day.

OLGA

"We had no dog to warn us if someone approached our house, so Mother selected the smartest of her new brood of ducklings and trained him as a watch duck," Olga remembers. "Georgie was his name. When Father switched on the radio, Mother let Georgie roam free in the yard. He would strut back and forth along the garden walk, surveying his domain. If anyone came near our front gate, he took off at a fast waddle for our front door, quacking ferociously in retreat. At the first quack, Father turned off the radio. Bombings over Germany happened around the clock. Mom always made sure to take Georgie along with the ducklings, baby chicks, and baby rabbits into the cellar if American bombers appeared overhead at noon, or the RAF bombers if they arrived at 8 p.m."

By 1944, all England became a military and supply base for British, American, and Canadian troops preparing to cross the English Channel to France to attack Hitler's defenses. On June 6, 1944—D-Day—the Allied army of nearly a million men landed on the beaches of Normandy, in France. They met fierce resistance from German troops but eventually won the day. Hitler's Europe had been invaded.

The Allied armies had two objectives: to engage the main body of German troops in northern France and to surge south and east out of Normandy toward Paris.

Hitler ordered Paris burned to the ground, but the order was never carried out. French Resistance forces rose in revolt against the German troops still in the city. Allied soldiers arrived before the Germans could crush the rebellion and destroy the city. On August 25, 1944, Liberation night, Paris turned on all the street and monument lights, and for the first time since June 14, 1940, it once again became the "City of Light."

While Paris celebrated, the Allied invasion forces continued their march toward Berlin. Hitler rallied his best units for one last desperate attempt to stop them. The sudden surprise attack came in the Ardennes region of Belgium on December 16, 1944. German armies almost pushed through the American and British lines in what became known as the Battle of the Bulge. On Christmas Eve, tree branches in the Ardennes shimmered with strips of tinfoil intended to fool German radar, making the

Packets of chow are served to American infantrymen in the snow and cold during the Battle of the Bulge in Belgium, the largest land battle of the war. After six weeks of fighting, U.S. and British Armies pressed in from all directions to squash the "bulge" where the Germans had pushed into the American front line.

forest look more like a Christmas card than a battleground. The Germans had Bastogne surrounded and ordered the Allies to surrender. Brigadier General McAuliffe's one-word response—"Nuts"—led to the biggest battle in U.S. Army history. Bastogne was rescued the day after Christmas by General Patton's tanks. Hitler had sacrificed 120,000 to 200,000 of his best soldiers. There were no replacements.

In addition to Allied armies, Resistance forces fought against Hitler in every country, including around Solange Berger's house in Belgium.

SOLANGE — "An American plane crash-landed near my house," Solange remembers. "It was a snowy day and the plane took our chimney, and a part of our ceiling fell on us. The American flyers were rescued by the Resistance people who hid them. When the Germans came to find the crew, no one would tell what they knew."

One of the German officers who lived in her house told her, "Fraulein, it is kaput. Germany is finished." Then he left and was killed that same day by the Resistance.

In February 1945, General Eisenhower, Supreme Commander of the Allied Forces in Europe, directed a massive advance toward Berlin.

The Russian Army was eager to get to Berlin first. They wanted revenge for the millions of Russians the Nazis had killed and for the unspeakable atrocities they had committed during the fighting in Russia. They wanted to fly their flag high above the roof of the Nazi Parliament building.

The end was near, but Hitler would not yield. He called all his remaining troops back to Berlin. The Berlin streets above the concrete bunker where he was hiding echoed with the sounds of Russian boots. To Adolf Hitler, surrender was unthinkable. He couldn't bear the thought of being captured, so he committed suicide by swallowing cyanide pills.

The final street fight of the war was exceptionally brutal. Hitler's Secret Service (S.S.) officers, alongside his Youth Groups, fought to the end for their führer.

 FRED — Fred Losch, part of Hitler Youth since age ten, was now attached to the First Officers Battalion of the Luftwaffe. His unit had new orders. "All forces were to go to Berlin to 'save our führer.' Morale was excellent. We were ready to fight and die for him,"

Fred says of his unit. "My group were all young cadets, with no war experience. As we traveled toward Berlin, the train stopped several times for air raids. Food was scarce. Word came that our commanding officer had been killed. We had no supplies, no ammunition, no artillery, no air cover, and no leader. We left the train and decided to keep walking toward Berlin and report to some organization.

"Every little group fought as well as it could. Confusion reigned. As we were dodging bullets and shrapnel, we heard the führer had died. Then later, we heard Germany had surrendered. We didn't want to surrender to Russia. If we had to surrender, we hoped to make it to the American or British forces.

"We were resting in the ditches alongside the road to keep a low profile. We heard a continuous whistling of bullets over our heads fired from a machine gun somewhere in the distance."

Fred and his group were surrounded. Most of his group decided it was time to stop. "I took my pistol, threw away the bolt, put sand in it and handed it to an enemy soldier.

"I was crying. I wept, and thought to myself, 'All this effort—for nothing.' I was a prisoner of war captured by Russia's Red Army." Fred Losch was only 17. The war in Europe was over.

On May 2, 1945, two days after Hitler's suicide, a Soviet soldier scales the roof of the German Parliament to raise the Soviet flag in victory over the Nazis. Below, Berlin lies in ruins. The Soviets reveled in the honor of capturing Hitler's capital.

29

Children in Hawaii reading the *Honolulu Star-Bulletin* on December 8, 1941, the day after the surprise attack on Pearl Harbor and the day when President Roosevelt asked Congress to declare war on Japan.

CHAPTER 3 ——————————— # war comes to the pacific

Before Hitler ever launched his campaign to conquer Europe, Japan had begun expanding its empire in Asia. Its savage invasion of China in 1940 alarmed the United States. President Roosevelt wanted Japan to realize that it was risking war with the United States if it continued its aggression against other countries. He ordered the U.S. fleet and other support services to move from California to Pearl Harbor, Hawaii. Japan saw this as a threat to its ambitions.

Events in Europe soon forced Roosevelt to transfer part of the fleet to the Atlantic as a show of support to countries fighting Hitler. This move left the Pacific fleet weakened. When Japan continued to push into French Indochina, the U.S. retaliated by stopping the sale of oil to Japan, freezing Japanese assets in U.S. banks, and closing U.S. ports to Japanese shipping. Japan realized that to continue expanding its empire it would have to defeat the United States. The countdown for an attack on Pearl Harbor had begun.

THOMPSON IZAWA, December 1941, Pearl City Peninsula, Oahu, Hawaii

Twelve-year-old Thompson Izawa loved fishing in Pearl Harbor with his father, Tsuneki, who was born in Japan. Thompson, American-born in Hawaii, was named for a Dr. Thompson, who saved his dad's life in a Honolulu shipyard accident. Thompson was proud to have an American name.

Thompson Izawa with his bike

December 7, 1941, began as any other Sunday for Thompson. He and his dad strapped fishing poles and line to dull black handlebars and pedaled off to their favorite fishing spot in the harbor. Thompson squinted at the battleship U.S.S. *Utah* outlined against the early sun. He and his dad baited the small squirming shrimp to fishhooks.

In the west, between the mountains and the ocean horizon, moving black specks enlarged into view. "It sounded like the hum of bees swarming," recalls Thompson. "Hundreds of airplanes were speeding toward us. As my dad and I sat there, we heard a high-pitched whistle

The Japanese Empire in World War II

ALASKA (U.S.)

Bering Sea

UNION OF SOVIET SOCIALIST REPUBLICS (SOVIET UNION)

Sea of Okhotsk (U.S.S.R.)

Kamchatka Peninsula

Aleutian Islands

Attu (U.S.)
Kiska

50°N

⊛ Urga
OUTER MONGOLIA

MANCHUKUO (MANCHURIA) (Japan)

Sakhalin I. (Japan)

Hokkaido

N O R T H

C H I N A

CHOSEN (KOREA) (Japan)

Sea of Japan

Honshu

⊛ Tokyo **JAPAN**

Shikoko

P A C I F I C

40°N

AFGHANISTAN
⊛ Kabul

TIBET
⊛ Lhasa

Delhi ⊛   Katmandu ⊛   ⊛ Punaka
NEPAL   **BHUTAN**

⊛ Chungking

East China Sea

Kyushu

O C E A N

Midway Is. (U.S.)

Hawaiian Islands

30°N

I N D I A (Great Britain)

BURMA (Gt. Br.)

Hong Kong (Gt. Br.)

● Macau (Port.)

FORMOSA (TAIWAN) (Japan)

Wake I. (U.S.)

HAWAII (U.S.)

20°N

Rangoon ⊛
⊛ Hanoi
FRENCH

Marianas Islands
(Japan)

Bay of

THAILAND
Bangkok ⊛

INDOCHINA (Fr.)

South China

Manila ● **PHILIPPINES** (U.S.)

Guam (U.S.)

Marshall Islands (Japan)

10°N

Colombo ⊛
CEYLON (Gt. Br.)

Bengal

(Gt. Br.) *Sea*

Sandakan
N. BORNEO (Gt. Br.)

Caroline Islands (Japan)

MALAY STATES
⊛ Singapore

BRUNEI
SARAWAK
⊛ Kuching
Borneo

EQUATOR

Sumatra

NETHERLANDS INDIES (Neth.)

NORTHEAST NEW GUINEA (Aust.)

Solomon Islands

EQUATOR

0°

Batavia ⊛

Java

(Port.)

New Guinea

PAPUA (Aust.)

(Gt. Br.)

10°S

I N D I A N

Timor Sea

New Hebrides (Gt. Br. & Fr.)

S O U T H

20°S

O C E A N

AUSTRALIA

Coral Sea

Fiji (Great Britain)

New Caledonia (France)

P A C I F I C

30°S

Canberra ⊛

O C E A N

◻ Greatest extent of the Japanese Empire, 6 August 1942

⊛ National or colonial capital

(Neth.) Country in control prior to the outbreak of World War II

Tasman Sea

NEW
⊛ Wellington
ZEALAND

40°S

ABBREVIATIONS
Aust............Australia
Fr................France
Gt. Br.........Great Britian
Neth............Netherlands
Port............Portugal
U.S..............United States
U.S.S.R.......Soviet Union

0   miles   1500
0   kilometers   2000

70°E   80°E   90°E   100°E   110°E   120°E   130°E   140°E   150°E   160°E   170°E   180°   170°W   160°W

and then saw the torpedo that slid through the water and blew up the battleship *Utah*. Not one American gun fired back.

"My dad grabbed me by my earlobe, 'Get home, boy. We are in big trouble—those are Japanese airplanes!' I wanted to stay and see the action, but my father took off pedaling for home.

"It was only three blocks to home, but already ten or more Japanese neighbors were waiting for my dad. Father had been in Hawaii the longest of the Japanese families—some 35 years. The neighbors relied on father, expecting him to explain what was happening. I remember first feeling proud of my papa-san, then excited by the hundreds of airplanes overhead, then fear about what might happen to my Japan-born parents."

Within three hours of the attack, a huge Navy troop truck squeaked to a stop in front of Thompson's house. Out jumped a soldier holding a megaphone and yelling at everyone to get in the truck. Three other soldiers with fixed bayonets surrounded the scared families, herding them into the large open-sided vehicle. The transport, overfilled with terrified Japanese civilians, seesawed up the hilly road to the sugarcane fields above Pearl Harbor.

That night, some 40 Japanese evacuees from Pearl City Peninsula slept on a dirt trail surrounded by tall grass and under guard of American soldiers. It rained most of the night. The next day, the Japanese families were allowed to take shelter indoors at a Buddhist church.

The attack on Pearl Harbor took everyone by surprise, especially the military.

JUDY RHOADES, December 7, 1941, Honolulu, Hawaii

On December 7, 1941, six-year-old Judy Rhoades and her younger sister lived about ten miles away from Pearl Harbor on a green hillside in a valley above Honolulu. Unexplained noises, distant booms, and the buzz of airplanes drew the girls out the kitchen door to the back porch. Judy remembers seeing a small plane disappear in a puff of black smoke. "We thought it was a tag game as we watched planes dip and twist in the skies over Pearl Harbor and Hickam Field. Our dad heard us and came out onto the porch. He told us, 'Get inside, now!'

"He herded us and Mom into the kitchen and turned on the radio. The insistent message stated, 'All military personnel report to duty stations immediately.' My father, an active-duty Navy carpenter with more than 20 years of service, didn't say much. He just hurriedly changed

Judy Rhoades (left), her mom, and her sister Dotty

33

Months before December 7, 1941, Japan designed a special torpedo that could dart through the shallow waters of Pearl Harbor. On December 7, Japanese bombers (left) dived to a low altitude and released torpedoes and bombs against America's great battleships. Fortunately, U.S. aircraft carriers were away at sea.

into khakis. He hugged us tight and told us to listen to our mother. Our mom must have been terrified for him to go into a war zone, but she kept any fear to herself. She bravely walked Dad to the car, told him to be careful, and then sent him off with a kiss.

"In the afternoon, the governor of Hawaii declared martial law. Before dark, our neighbor was appointed warden for our area. He asked my mother to be prepared with weapons and have them in easy reach in case the Japanese invaded. My mother put a hammer, meat cleaver, and a butcher knife on the dining room table. The warden's second instruction was to maintain a total blackout. 'Not even a sliver of light can shine out of this house,' he warned us. Thirdly, he told us to watch the skies for enemy paratroopers. My sister and I were given the job of looking for anything resembling an umbrella coming down. The watch was to last until the next morning. Mom brought us milk and cookies to help us stay awake.

"We didn't see Daddy for two days. When he got home, his uniform was dirty and torn. He showered, then slept deeply for several hours. In the back seat of his car were stacks of white towels. We were adults before we found out those towels were to pick up body parts of those who had been maimed or killed at Pearl Harbor."

Oily black smoke billows up from the stricken U.S.S. *Arizona* during Japan's second attack wave. American guns explode bursts of antiaircraft shells dotting overhead skies. This photo was taken from the nearby hills where civilians watched in fear and disbelief.

Everyone was required to be fingerprinted and carry their identification card with them at all times. Most children attached them to a cord and wore them around their necks.

Children around the world played endless games of war. In Ewa, Hawaii, this "barefoot army" of American children of Japanese ancestry executes "present arms" with "guns" of sticks, bamboo, and wood.

All over Hawaii, schools were canceled immediately to prepare for wartime conditions. It took two and a half months to build bomb shelters at every school. Students lined up to get shots to prepare for germ warfare. Thousands of gas masks had to come by ship and then be distributed. Identification cards showing fingerprints and blood type were required for everyone. Also required was an exchange of American currency for invasion money. The banks printed "Hawaii" on both sides of paper money so if the Japanese invaded Hawaii they wouldn't be able to use American cash to buy weapons or supplies in other countries.

JUDY — "I was so disappointed when school closed," says Judy Rhoades. "That meant no Christmas play. I was to be Mary, and the only first-grade performer.

"Daddy dug a bomb shelter in the front yard, but our valley got a lot of rain, and being on a downhill slope, it filled with water. My sister and I would catch frogs in it. When the air raid sirens blared, we went to the shelter across the street, which was in a higher yard.

"When school finally re-opened in mid-February, dug-out slits in the ground called bomb trenches zigzagged across our playground. To practice for a possible air raid, we had to jump down into the trenches and crouch with hands over our heads. For poison gas practice, our teachers asked us to hold our breath while securing our masks. We thought we looked like alien anteaters with them on. Sometimes, we had to giggle when we looked at each other. Our teacher, Mrs. Barber, would give us a lecture about being serious.

"We played endless games of war, choosing up sides and trying to capture the other team's hidden flag. We learned to listen and follow directions and routines, like getting my lunch box, gas mask, ID card, dog tag, and schoolbooks before going to school. I did well with all routines except the air raid sirens. I'll never forget the sound; eerie, insistent, shrill, scary.

"Because of the fear of another attack, thousands of wives and children shipped out of Hawaii on military troop ships. In April 1942, Mom, my little sister, and I were among hundreds of mothers and children evacuated to the safety of mainland America. We traveled in a convoy, encircled by a protective military escort of submarines, armed soldiers, and warships. It was horrible to say good-bye to Daddy not knowing when we would be together again."

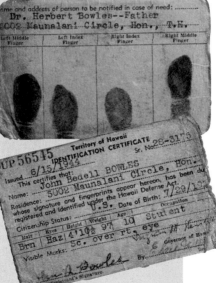

Martial law in Hawaii required the registration and fingerprinting of all civilians over the age of six.

Within hours of bombing Pearl Harbor, swarms of Japanese planes struck nearly every major American installation on Luzon, the Philippines' largest island. As a commonwealth of the United States, the Philippines relied on the U.S. for its defense.

Caught off guard, the Philippines became the second Pearl Harbor. U.S. planes parked on the ground at Clark Field wingtip to wingtip made easy targets for the bombs of Japanese Zeros. The United States had been beaten twice in one day. Within two days, the Japanese invaded the Philippines. Within ten days, their troops marched toward Manila and took prisoners, both military and civilian.

Joyce ("Joy") Louise Crichton with her amah Carmen and old friend Tailey (below)

JOYCE ("JOY") LOUISE CRICHTON,
December 1941, Manila, Philippines

Before Japan attacked Pearl Harbor and the Philippines, Joyce ("Joy") Louise Crichton and her older sister, Carol, lived a peaceful carefree life in the British section of Manila. Her father's job as an accountant for an import-export firm provided the family with a gracious way of living. She and her sister were too young to be afraid or worry what might happen to them when Manila surrendered to the Japanese in January 1942. "We had servants so my mother didn't have to know how to cook or drive, and I loved Carmen Garfil, my Filipino *amah* [nanny]," says Joy. "I remember my wonderful second birthday when all my friends came with their amahs and brought me presents. My favorite was a tan and brown stuffed squirrel made of smooth Indian-head cotton. It was from my friend Pinkie. I named him 'Tailey.'

"Japanese officers arrived at our house in early January. They decided they liked our house and declared it their troop headquarters. Mother, father, my sister Carol, and myself were ordered to leave immediately and take only one suitcase. Everything else in the house, including our new Pontiac sedan, now belonged to the Imperial Japanese Army. We hugged tearful good-byes to our Filipino servants and our beloved Carmen. Before we went out the door, Mom tucked Tailey, my favorite toy, into my suitcase.

"Soldiers transported us to Santo Tomas University on January 9, 1942. The campus, with its dorms, classrooms, and high stone wall barriers, was an obvious choice for an internment camp. At first everyone slept in classrooms lined with wall-to-wall beds. Later the men and women were separated at night. Father slept on a hammock jammed against thousands of

others in the men's dorm in the gymnasium. So we could be together as a family in the daytime, Dad scavenged wood and straw pieces to build us a *nipa* [a hut or shanty].

"One night in the Santo Tomas camp, I had been fighting with my friend Tonya, who took Tailey and wouldn't tell what she had done with him. Mom came in the room and turned on the lights, violating camp blackout rules. Mom demanded the squirrel be returned now, or the light would stay on, assuring the wrath of the Japanese guards, who had recently killed a man trying to escape from camp. Tonya confessed, and Mom scrambled up onto the roof and snatched Tailey off the ledge. I didn't find out until after the war why Mom was so upset. Before the Japanese forced us out of our house, she had pulled out most of Tailey's cotton filling and restuffed him with jewelry and tightly rolled currency!"

At the Santo Tomas camp, all the men slept on cots or hammocks in the gym (above). Women and children had iron bunk beds in classrooms. Sheets draped over clotheslines provided some privacy.

"The biggest problem in the camp was hunger. Breakfast was watery mush thickened with coconut milk. Lunch was always the same, slimy spinach, beans, rice, sweet potatoes. Dinner, sometimes a very thin black soup. Women traded huge diamond rings for tiny containers of milk. My father traded his silver cigarette lighter for food for us. He was grateful his camp job was to work in the kitchen so he could sneak out potato peelings to us.

"I remember my mother hoarding money to buy eggs so she could bake me a birthday cake over an open fire. The money was smuggled to my mother by Carmen, my former amah, who had always called me her baby. When our clothes went out to be washed, Carmen hid the money in the sashes of our dresses, risking her own life to help our family.

"I'll never forget Liberation Day, February 3, 1945. In the afternoon, six American planes flew low and slow so that we could see them clearly. The camp went mad, cheering and waving, realizing this was finally freedom day. The Japanese panicked, soldiers armed with fixed bayonets ran around trying to force us back into the buildings. Giving up, they quickly barricaded themselves in the Education Building.

In a dramatic rescue on February 3, 1945, U.S. Army soldiers liberated 3,500 prisoners of war from the Santo Tomas internment camp. Joy (on the right), along with her mom and sister, had been imprisoned for 39 months.

"I can still see the green flare and then American tanks smashing through the walls as a roar went up from all of us. Seven hundred U.S. soldiers of the Army First Cavalry regiment with the 24th Tank Battalion commanded by General Chase were our liberators. I asked one of the big Americans his name. Kneeling down, he smiled, 'Leonard.' 'Thank you, Leonard,' I whispered."

After three years in a Philippine internment camp, Joy and her family were free and safe.

But in Japan there were no safe areas, especially in Tokyo. In early 1944, heavy bombing had not yet reached Japan's homeland. This changed when the U.S. captured the island of Saipan in July. From there, the land-based B-29s could easily reach Japan. By March 1945, the air raids on Tokyo intensified.

Eiko Arai with brother, Ichitaro

EIKO ARAI, March 1945, Tokyo, Japan Twelve-year-old Eiko Arai lived in Tokyo with her mother, Taka, and her younger brother, Ichitaro. Her father, Hikichi, had been drafted into the Japanese Army. This left her mother alone to take care of Eiko and Ichitaro. The Arai family was well-to-do, with a two-story tile-roof house in Tokyo and a country house a short train ride away in Takasaki.

"March 1945 was the beginning of the most difficult part of the war for me when the bombings were almost daily," recalls Eiko. "We spent a lot of time rushing into our bomb shelter in our yard. I didn't like the foul smell of the damp dirt, and the creeping, crawling bugs scared me.

"Our mother, sewed a *bokuzukin,* which was a padded hood covering the head and shoulders against flying shrapnel pieces. Mother put this into a bag with a strap that held underwear, the name and address of family to notify, and sometimes a snack. Some mothers painted their child's name and blood type on their chest, but our mother pinned a nametag to our clothes, noting blood type. Every time the air raid sirens sounded, we grabbed the bag. In the shelter, she stored peanuts for protein, salt, water in a barrel, and an apple for moisture and fiber if she could get one.

"When the first siren sounded, it meant the B-29s were on their way and to prepare to go to the shelter. There were two different sounds. When the pitch changed, it meant the B-29s were over the city. If we didn't get to the shelter in time and a bomb hit nearby, we felt lifted up

When the U.S. captured the islands of Saipan, Tinian, and Guam, American bombers were within striking range of Tokyo. On March 9, 1945, 300 B-29s dropped 2,000 tons of bombs on Tokyo. Eiko and her family escaped from the bombs and the fires that killed 84,000 people.

from the house as the bomb exploded. Sometimes it was hours after a bombing before we could leave the shelter because the air outside was so thick with smoke and dust.

"Following a period of day raids, the frightening night raids began. On the night of March 9, 1945, the sirens blared. We dressed in the dark, grabbed our packed 'emergency bag,' and raced down the staircase for the bomb shelter. Leaving the house, I looked back toward our upstairs. It was gone, but a man's leg had blown against our house and was wedged into the burning staircase still wearing one shoe.

"Outdoors, the entire sky glowed yellow-red. Tokyo was on fire, torched by firebombs which descended out of the B-29s in beautiful but deadly showers. Upon impact, trees and bushes lit up like Christmas trees, turning the night as bright as day. The fire circled the city, burning and destroying as it moved toward the center of Tokyo.

"Most people tried to escape the approaching fires by running in the opposite direction;

toward the center of the city. The circle of fire eventually reached them. Thousands who hid in bomb shelters died from lack of oxygen. Tokyo smoldered in total ruins.

"My mother knew she had to take us through the approaching fire to save us. Mama-san tied my brother and me to herself, to pull us through the smoke. To protect us crossing through fire, she covered us with a wet blanket.

"We stepped over charred bodies as we moved away from the city, always stepping into the wind while heading to the train station on the other side of the fires.

"The windows on the railroad cars were blown out, but some trains were still operating. Hundreds of people were jammed into rail cars, standing up on the seats, children on shoulders, anything to squeeze in one more person. The door closed, and the train started up before I could board. My mom screamed and a kind man reached out and pulled me in with both hands. There were so many of us in the train standing on top of each other that my head kept bobbing against the ceiling as we rolled down the tracks toward Takasaki and our country house.

"We hoped that living in the country close to farmers we would have food. But the farmers wouldn't sell their food for money. Instead they asked for our family heirlooms and valuable possessions. To obtain food for our family we traded beautiful embroidered silk kimonos. When we had no more valuables, Mother went to the fields to gather sweet potato vines to cook and boil for us to eat. I still can't eat sweet potatoes today, but I don't ever waste food.

"On August 6, 1945, the American bomber 'Enola Gay' dropped the first atomic bomb on Hiroshima, and another three days later on Nagasaki. The use of this strange and powerful bomb was ordered by U.S. President Truman. It was only reported sparingly in the Tokyo paper, and I didn't have any personal experience with it.

"On August 15, 1945—V-J Day—we all listened to the radio to hear our emperor speak to us. It was the first time he spoke directly to the people. In an emotional voice he said it was time for Japan to surrender. Afterward we all bowed; some cried. I don't remember if I did. Many men felt responsible for not saving our emperor. Some went off alone to commit suicide using a sword or knife to die quickly. The expression is that 'they died clean and with distinction.' They were not bent over and did not cry out in suffering. They were loyal to the emperor. This *harakiri* [ritual suicide] was to atone for their role in Japan's defeat."

The surrender document was signed in Tokyo Bay on September 2, 1945.

The "Join the Schools at War Program" urged children to collect scrap metal, rubber, paper, fat, silk, and nylon for recycling into war weapons. These students in Hawaii perform their patriotic duty by salvaging scrap metal for "Uncle Sam."

CHAPTER 3 —————— home front america

In war there is the battle front where the soldiers fight, and the home front where civilians join together to support the troops. For millions of children of World War II, their home front was the battle front. The ones who suffered most were the children of Europe and Asia. The experience in America, which was isolated by the Atlantic and Pacific Oceans, was vastly different.

JAMES J. FISHER, December 7, 1941, Kansas City, Missouri

On the mainland of the United States, December 7, 1941, was like any other Sunday. Five-year-old James J. Fisher sprawled on the floor next to the big upright Philco radio. He thumbed through the comic pages of his dad's newspaper.

"I vaguely remember something coming over the radio when my father, the smartest man I ever knew, said, 'Son, this is important—remember this.' And I did remember, In all the years we had that Philco, no matter how exciting the *Lone Ranger* or *The Shadow* got, I couldn't look at it and not remember Pearl Harbor and the afternoon when everything changed."

James Fisher (right) and brother Mike wearing "bomber caps"

The next day President Roosevelt asked Congress for a declaration of war against Japan. It took only 33 minutes for Congress to vote "yes."

An outraged America geared up to fight the most devastating global war in modern history. Every home in America either sent someone off to war or personally knew someone away in the war. President Roosevelt asked all those on the home front to support their fighting men by writing letters to them, working in war plants, and making sacrifices. Tires, cars, washing machines, shoes, sugar, butter, meat, and women's stockings were just some of what Americans willingly did with less of or did without.

James Fisher, then a first grader, recalls, "I had no problem when elastic all but disappeared because our Army needed rubber. It meant I had to 'sacrifice' wearing the knickers I hated. Instead I got to wear pants to school. At school and home, war also changed the way we played.

"We played guns and war. We wore aviator caps and steel helmets. Even on tricycles we were pilots or soldiers. We saved tinfoil off our gum, and collected tires and newspapers, and carted our bacon grease to a big red, white, and blue box behind our elementary school. [Fats were needed to make glycerin, an essential ingredient in explosives.]

"At the grocery store, the metal can of maple syrup shaped like a log cabin disappeared from the shelves. My mother spent hours figuring out the best way to use the tiny ration stamps, and she and my father had to wait in long lines to purchase their two packs of Chesterfield cigarettes.

"Some things as a kid I didn't understand, like the woman in the drugstore who picked up glassware and smashed it to floor. When the clerk rushed over, spoke with her, then joined in the breaking, I asked my mother why. 'Made in Japan,' she explained."

Americans openly displayed hatred against the Japanese. Movies, posters, newspapers, and cartoons all encouraged and accepted the racial degrading. No one wanted to be accused of being a "Jap lover." When President Roosevelt issued executive order #9066 on February 18, 1942, and established the War Relocation Authority (WRA) on March 18, 1942, forcing all Japanese living on the West Coast to give up their homes, few Americans objected. U.S. Army soldiers tacked up posters notifying residents they were to be evacuated even though most were American-born.

Allan Hida (left) with his mother, Hide, and brother Ed at Amache Camp, Colorado

Allan's ID tag

"On May 8, 1942, the signs went up and we were to be gone," recalls Allan Hida, then a seventh grader living near Sacramento. "My father was required to register our little family and then get us our identification tags to wear during the evacuation process. We had to leave everything behind, taking only what few approved personal items we could carry. My mother's camera was not approved and was snatched from her. No pets of any kind were allowed.

By the first anniversary of the Pearl Harbor attack, every Japanese man, woman, and child on the U.S. West Coast was forced to leave their homes. More than two-thirds were American born citizens—mostly infants, children, and teenagers. The refugees could take only what they could carry, leaving behind their homes, businesses, farmland, and pets. To help keep their dignity, this couple wears their best clothes as they say good-bye to their dog.

"Drab brown Army trucks hauled us to Walerga, a temporary evacuation center near Sacramento. Thousands of Japanese were confined in temporary assembly centers like this one, while waiting for permanent relocation (WRA) camps to be built."

By the first anniversary of the Pearl Harbor attack, every man, woman, and child of Japanese ancestry on the West Coast—more than 110,000—was imprisoned in a WRA camp. To isolate the Japanese Americans from major cities, all the WRA camps were built in desolate parts of the country. Barbed wire encircled the compound grounds. Overhead, armed guards positioned themselves in watchtowers. Searchlights roamed the night sky.

"Right after my 13th birthday, we were sent to remote Tule Lake high in the mountains of northern California," Allan remembers. "Because of the high altitude, we endured winters of minus 25 degrees Fahrenheit [-30°C] in drafty, cramped barracks. Attempts at school studies

There were nearly 30,000 school-age children in the internment camps and a shortage of books, teachers, and classrooms. There were no school supplies. This grieved Japanese parents, who valued education and always encouraged their children to be good students.

were a joke. We lacked everything: paper, books, blackboards, teachers. Then, my grandfather Hida died while we were forced to live in that barren isolation."

The Hida family's final move took them to the Amache relocation center on the dry plains of southeast Colorado. The rattlesnakes and prairie dogs were a friendlier welcome than the JAPS NOT WANTED sign posted at a nearby town.

While the Japanese Americans were confined to camps, other home front Americans were benefiting financially from the war. Americans who were hungry and jobless before the war were now needed by the thousands to work in war plants. American factories hummed round-the-clock to supply the war front.

Thousands of willing workers moved close to factories to produce the war

Tule Lake internees attend the funeral of Allan's grandfather outside their desolate barracks. Allan is standing behind the left end of the casket. There were ten different internment camps scattered in isolated areas in the West. Each housed about 10,000 people.

machines and weapons that made America's eight million fighting men the best-equipped army in the world. Women answered the call to fill the jobs vacated by the men away at the battle fronts.

Dora Mae Boone, high-school graduation picture

DORA MAE BOONE, January 1943, Wichita, Kansas

When 17-year-old Dora Mae Boone completed the 12th grade in 1942, she hoped to go to nursing school, but there was a war on. The boys were all going off to fight and her friends were going to work in the war plants. Dora could hardly wait until she was old enough to be hired. As soon as she turned 18, she moved to Wichita, Kansas, to become a "Rosie" at the former Coleman Lamp and Stove Company, now converted to a war plant.

"My job was very exacting with a lot of handwork. I worked on the rotor that went into making machine gun pellets. It doesn't sound like an art, but they all had to be inspected to be sure there was no flaw in them."

Dora was one of the millions of women who worked in the factories during the war. The label "Rosie the Riveter" became the catchall name for all the women in defense work. These women were the ones who built the tanks, planes, and ships being used by our boys "over there." Undoubtedly the most famous "Rosie" was Norma Jean Baker, a young brunette working in an airplane plant whose photo was widely published. Everyone wanted to know who she was. After the war she changed her hair color to blond and her name to Marilyn Monroe and became a famous movie star.

As the war continued, families who pledged their wholehearted support were presented with a "V Home" poster to place in the front window. It meant the family had recycled everything possible, prepared for emergencies, knew their local air raid warden, kept phone calls brief to keep lines clear for military use, and grew their own vegetables so that farm goods could be sent to the war front. These "victory gardens" began to appear in backyards across the country.

Posters like this recruited women to work in defense plants to free up the men to go to war. The women responded, wanting to be patriotic but also wanting the higher pay. World War II was the real beginning of women working outside the home.

People on the home front also supported the war effort by buying savings bonds.

Betty Jo (right) and friends in a jeep

BETTY JO OETTING, October 1942, Raytown, Missouri

"I sometimes did without lunch or milk to buy savings bonds stamps to lick and stick in my stamp book," recalls Betty Jo Oetting, then a ten-year-old fifth grader. "By buying a few stamps at a time, even kids like me could help with the war. My dad was school superintendent. He convinced two soldiers with an Army jeep to come to our school and give a ride around the playground to any student who bought a war bond. I really wanted a ride in that jeep. I saved $18.75 worth of dimes to fill my stamp book so I could get that ride. Well, I got the ride and more. Dad invited those soldiers to a home-cooked meal at our house. Of course, they accepted. Before dinner, my friends and I squeezed ourselves into that jeep and squealed at every bump and hole as we bounced over the countryside, all over our neighborhood, not just the school grounds."

Dorinda, the author, at age 6

DORINDA MAKANAŌNALANI STAGNER, January 1943, Pearl City, Hawaii

"In Hawaii, we could grow vegetables year-round. My job was to hoe the weeds, and I hated it. I complained, and when that didn't work, I pouted. For punishment, I wasn't allowed to go to the Saturday afternoon movie, which was the major fun of the week for children during the war.

"Because we also had a meat shortage, my dad said we were going to grow another crop that he called 'Pearl City Chicken.' Dad built wooden cages above the ground, called hutches. He bought some rabbits, and I eventually learned they were to be our new food source for the family. But not for me.

"The rabbits were an Angora breed with lots of black and white fluffy fur. I named the first one Patches and called his mate Mrs. Patches. I also named all of their babies. To save the rabbits, I began to hoe the garden and pull weeds without complaining. And I even learned to like vegetables."

In December 1944, three years after Pearl Harbor, the (WRA) relocation camps ended as they had begun, by orders from President Roosevelt. Not one Japanese American (AJA) was ever convicted of sabotage against the United States. Surprisingly, many AJA citizens who had been imprisoned solely because of their race now volunteered to fight as American soldiers.

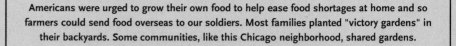

Americans were urged to grow their own food to help ease food shortages at home and so farmers could send food overseas to our soldiers. Most families planted "victory gardens" in their backyards. Some communities, like this Chicago neighborhood, shared gardens.

DORINDA— On April 12, 1945, only a few months before the war's end, President Roosevelt died. He was the only American President I had ever known. "Mrs. Taylor, my fifth-grade teacher, cried as she circled our class under the school flagpole. Our principal unwound the faded gray cords from the pole. Slowly, hand-over-hand, he lowered the flag to half-mast as our voices blended into 'God bless America, Land that I love…'

"Mom thought she should cancel her hula classes on August 14, 1945, when our new President, Harry Truman, announced Japan's surrender. But her students wanted to celebrate and be together. Mom agreed to provide rides home after class. It was dark when our '39 Ford sedan packed with giggling girls angled onto the main road.

"Suddenly firecrackers exploded all around us. Mom sounded her horn, and with windows down and waving hands outstretched, we inched our way through the ecstatic celebration. Children paraded while clanging pots and pans together, chanting, 'The war is over.' We could

Searchlights that previously had scanned skies over Pearl Harbor for enemy planes now join flares, ships' whistles, firework rockets, and arcs of water sprayed from fire boats in a thunderous celebration on the evening of August 14, 1945, V-J Day.

see fireworks from the harbor, and air raid sirens wailed along with the gonging of gas alarms.

"The sky over the harbor flashed with flares. The night air was filled with every mixture of ships' whistles, from small tugboats to giant battleships, adding their voices to the sirens and gongs. In a spontaneous eruption of joy and excitement, people hugged and kissed anyone next to them.

"Mom guided our black Ford into a right turn, returning home to quiet Jean Street, where we lived. Our car lights picked up the white uniform of a young sailor standing in the yard across from our house. Unlike those who were celebrating, he was alone. With his back to me, he leaned his forearm into the curve of a palm tree, and cradled his face in the bend of his elbow. I didn't hear him cry, but I could see his shoulders and head quake with emotion. I realize now that I was witnessing the private ceremony of a young sailor, thousands of miles from home, who realized he had managed to survive."

Finally, after four long years, the war was over for America.

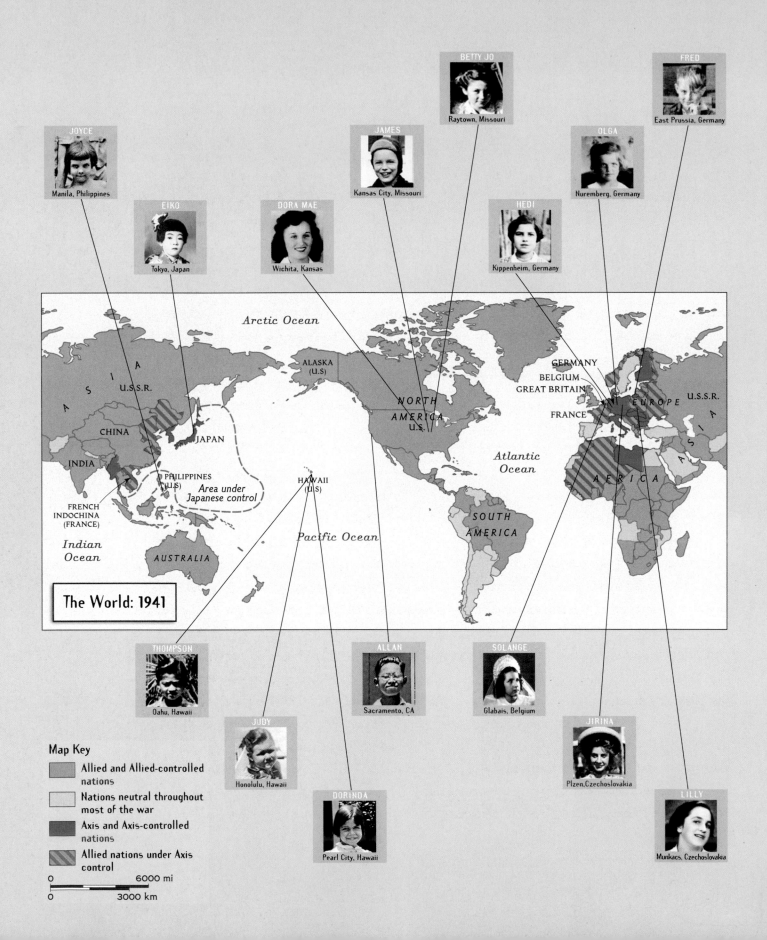

JOYCE
Manila, Philippines

EIKO
Tokyo, Japan

DORA MAE
Wichita, Kansas

JAMES
Kansas City, Missouri

BETTY JO
Raytown, Missouri

HEDI
Kippenheim, Germany

OLGA
Nuremberg, Germany

FRED
East Prussia, Germany

THOMPSON
Oahu, Hawaii

JUDY
Honolulu, Hawaii

DORINDA
Pearl City, Hawaii

ALLAN
Sacramento, CA

SOLANGE
Glabais, Belgium

JIRINA
Plzen, Czechoslovakia

LILLY
Munkacs, Czechoslovakia

Arctic Ocean

ALASKA
(U.S)

A S I A

U.S.S.R.

CHINA

JAPAN

INDIA

PHILIPPINES
(U.S)

Area under
Japanese control

HAWAII
(U.S)

FRENCH
INDOCHINA
(FRANCE)

Indian
Ocean

AUSTRALIA

Pacific Ocean

NORTH
AMERICA
U.S.

GERMANY
BELGIUM
GREAT BRITAIN

FRANCE

EUROPE

U.S.S.R.

A S I A

AFRICA

Atlantic
Ocean

SOUTH
AMERICA

The World: 1941

Map Key

Allied and Allied-controlled
nations

Nations neutral throughout
most of the war

Axis and Axis-controlled
nations

Allied nations under Axis
control

0   6000 mi

0   3000 km

epilogue

No other event of the 20th century was as momentous or as hideous as World War II. More civilians were killed than soldiers. No one suffered more than the children, especially those of the Holocaust. By 1946, there were practically no children between the ages of six and twelve among the displaced Jews in Germany. In other parts of Europe and Asia, orphans were left to fend for themselves in bombed-out cities.

The children who had survived the war now had to survive peacetime. There was filth, disease and shortages of everything, especially food. In Japan, Eiko's mother continued to scavenge sweet potato vines to boil and eat. She also boiled the family's clothes, which were infested with lice.

Lilly and her sister were liberated from Reichenbach, but there was no home or family waiting for them. The cruel hardships of war remained long after the surrender treaty was signed and before food and aid could be delivered to the starving survivors.

The kids you see pictured to the left in the global collage are in their sixties and seventies now. Each one is representative of the millions of children of war across the world. I am grateful to these few for telling their stories. I wish there was room to tell you all they shared with me. Stories such as Olga hanging a white sheet out her attic window to welcome the American tanks as they rolled into her village. Or, Lilly crying and kissing the ground when she first saw the Statue of Liberty. The stories from these vulnerable victims of war allow us to experience what it was like to be a child during World War II. So, to see the war through their eyes is what makes this history alive, personal, and compelling.

Today, all the "kids" are living fulfilling and productive lives. They realize daily problems are meaningless compared to the sacrifices of war. Although some still find the shrill sound of sirens frightening, they live with compassion and without hate.

This year marks the 60th anniversary of the end of World War II. Sadly, the opportunity to hear first-person stories from our veterans is fading away. Soon the only survivors who experienced the deadliest war in human history will be the children of the "greatest generation." These "kids" will be the last eyewitnesses to the futility and brutality of World War II.

If we want a lasting peace, we would do well to look to the children of war in every generation. They are wise beyond their years. They can tell us what war does to the human spirit. They have seen it up close.

WORLD WAR II TIME LINE

This time line shows some of the key events of the war in Europe (blue columns), on the Home Front (yellow columns), and in the Pacific (tan columns). Operations in Africa are commonly considered as part of the European theater. The Pacific theater included action on islands in the Pacific Ocean as well as on the mainland of Asia.

By the time war was declared in Europe, Adolf Hitler had already annexed the Rhineland, Austria, and part of Czechoslovakia. Meanwhile Japan was expanding its empire in Asia and the Pacific. By the time the Japanese attacked Pearl Harbor, they had occupied much of China and the eastern part of mainland Southeast Asia.

WAR IN EUROPE

In Europe, 20,000 orphans were left homeless by the war.

THE HOME FRONT

Posters encouraged Americans to plant victory gardens.

WAR IN THE PACIFIC

Children in Hawaii always had to carry gas masks.

1939

WAR IN EUROPE

AUGUST
The Soviet Union and Germany sign a nonaggression pact known as the Molotov-Ribbentrop Agreement in which the Soviets agree not to interfere with Hitler's plans to invade Poland.

SEPTEMBER
The Kindertransport program, which began after *Kristallnacht* in November 1938, moves 10,000 European refugee children—most of them Jewish—to England where they live with British families. The program ends in Germany just before Poland is invaded.

Hitler invades Poland as the German Army unleashes blitzkrieg, or "lightning warfare."

France and Great Britain declare war on Germany. World War II begins in Europe.

OCTOBER
Nazis begin persecuting Polish Jews.

NOVEMBER
Soviet Union invades Finland.

DECEMBER
Soviet Union is expelled from the League of Nations for attacking Finland.

THE HOME FRONT

SEPTEMBER
President Roosevelt issues Proclamation of Neutrality, promising to provide aid but not to send American troops to fight in Europe

DECEMBER
The U.S., which supplies most of Japan's aviation fuel, stops the export to Japan of technical information about the production of aviation fuel.

1940

WAR IN EUROPE

MARCH
Finland and the Soviet Union sign a peace treaty. The Finns retain their independence but lose territory.

APRIL
The German Army invades Denmark and Norway and soon conquers both.

MAY
Germany invades Belgium, the Netherlands, Luxembourg, and France.

The evacuation of the British Army from France at Dunkirk begins.

The Netherlands, Belgium, and Luxembourg fall to Hitler.

JUNE
Italy enters the war as Germany's ally.

France surrenders to Hitler's forces.

JULY
Britain rejects Hitler's peace pact. The Battle of Britain begins with German bombing raids over English Channel.

AUGUST
German air forces (Luftwaffe) attack southern England.

SEPTEMBER
The London Blitz begins as Germany launches a series of bombings that continues for 57 nights and claims the lives of more than 40,000 Londoners. Air raids over England continue until spring 1945.

OCTOBER
More than 400,000 Polish Jews are herded into a part of Warsaw known as the Warsaw Ghetto.

DECEMBER
Hitler plans to invade the Soviet Union.

THE HOME FRONT

APRIL
U.S. population reaches 131 million. Leaders look for ways to avoid war while aiding the forces of democracy.

JULY
The U.S. stops exports of scrap iron and steel to Japan.

NOVEMBER
Roosevelt is elected to an unprecedented third term as President.

WAR IN THE PACIFIC

JULY
Japan begins its advance into French Indochina on the mainland of Southeast Asia.

SEPTEMBER
Japan signs a pact allying it with Italy and Germany. The three countries are the chief members of the Axis powers.

1941

FEBRUARY
Germany and Spain sign a secret defensive pact.

APRIL
Germany invades and takes control of Greece and Yugoslavia.

JUNE
Germany invades the Soviet Union in Operation Barbarossa.

SEPTEMBER
The German Army lays siege to Leningrad (now St. Petersburg) in the Soviet Union.

OCTOBER
Germans attack Moscow. To date, the Soviet Union has lost 600,000 square miles of territory to the Germans.

DECEMBER
Soviets launch a counteroffensive to stop the German advance on Moscow.

Hitler declares war on the U.S.

MARCH
Franklin Roosevelt promises aid to countries fighting Germany until victory is achieved.

JULY
U.S. cuts off all oil exports to Japan.

OCTOBER
German submarine sinks the destroyer *Reuben James*. It is the first U.S. ship sunk in the European war. Roosevelt says the event will not affect German-American relations.

NOVEMBER
Talks between the U.S. and Japan break down.

DECEMBER
Japan attacks Pearl Harbor on December 7. One day later FDR signs a declaration of war against Japan. Americans by the millions sign up to fight. Volunteers can choose which branch of the military to join.

NOVEMBER
Japanese fleet secretly sets sail for Pearl Harbor.

DECEMBER
Japan attacks the U.S. naval base at Pearl Harbor and then Allied bases in the Philippines, Guam, Wake Island, Hong Kong, Malaya, and Singapore.

The U.S. declares war on Japan.

The Japanese defeat American forces on Guam and Wake Island.

Japanese troops invade the Philippines.

1942

JANUARY
The Wannsee Conference establishes the Nazi plan to exterminate the Jews.

MAY
German Army starts a third counteroffensive in North Africa.

AUGUST
German Army begins the Battle of Stalingrad (now Volgograd).

NOVEMBER
British Army's defeat of German Afrika Korps at El Alamein is a turning point in the war in North Africa.

Soviet forces break the siege of Stalingrad and counterattack, putting the Germans on the defensive.

JANUARY
War Production Board stops production of nonessentials, including refrigerators and lawnmowers. Controls are placed on rubber, metal, and silk. Children scavenge for anything metal or rubber to recycle.

FEBRUARY
Executive order #9066 begins the forced removal of all Japanese Americans from West Coast locations to internment camps.

APRIL
Rationing is enforced through the OPA (Office of Price Administration). Sugar is rationed first, then coffee.

MAY
Congress establishes the Women's Auxiliary Corp, later known as WAC (Women's Army Corp).

JUNE
Japanese troops land on Alaska's Aleutian Islands.

JULY
WAVES (Women Accepted for Voluntary Emergency Service) organize as U.S. Naval Reserve.

OCTOBER
Factories switch over to war production. Millions of women enter the workforce for the first time.

More than 20 million Americans plant "victory gardens.'

NOVEMBER
SPARS, the women's branch of the Coast Guard, is established.

APRIL
Lieutenant Colonel James Doolittle leads a surprise air raid on Tokyo.

MAY
Japan gains control of the Philippines.

JUNE
U.S. Navy wins the Battle of Midway.

1943

FEBRUARY
German Sixth Army surrenders at Stalingrad. This halts Hitler's advance eastward and marks a turning point in the war in Europe.

MAY
Axis forces surrender in North Africa, giving Allied armies control of bases from which to launch an invasion of southern Europe.

JULY
Soviet Army, advancing westward, defeats German Army at Kursk in the war's biggest tank battle.

Allies invade Sicily off the tip of Italy.

SEPTEMBER
Italy surrenders to the Allies.

British and American troops land at Salerno and begin to push their way up the Italian peninsula.

NOVEMBER
Allied forces reach Cassino, just south of Rome, and meet heavy resistance from the German Army.

JANUARY
War bonds are offered for sale. Children can buy a stamp for 10 cents, collect them in books, and eventually purchase a war bond for $18.75. In ten years the bond will be worth $25.00.

FEBRUARY
Leather shortage leads to shoe rationing, limiting Americans to three pairs per year per person.

MAY
U.S. forces end Japanese occupation in the Aleutian Islands.

JUNE
Office of War Information is established to control official news and propaganda.

DECEMBER
Short supply of gasoline leads to strict rationing, usually three gallons per week per family. To control price gouging, OPA limits the price of goods.

President Roosevelt asks Americans to win the war by making sacrifices. A shortage of fabric means shorter skirts and no ruffles or pockets. Without nylon for stockings, women paint their legs so it looks like they are wearing hose.

APRIL
Over Bougainville in the Solomon Islands U.S. air forces shoot down a plane carrying Admiral Yamamoto, the Japanese naval chief who planned the attack on Pearl Harbor.

1944

JANUARY
Siege of Leningrad ends. Soviet Army pushes German Army back to Poland.

APRIL
U.S. planes begin bombing Berlin, Germany's capital.

JUNE
American, British, and Canadian forces successfully land at Normandy on D-Day and begin their march inland to liberate Europe.

Allied forces liberate Rome.

AUGUST
Allies liberate Paris.

NOVEMBER
U.S. troops begin a drive to reach the Rhine River in Germany.

DECEMBER
Battle of the Bulge begins as the German Army attacks the Americans in the Ardennes Forest in Belgium.

OCTOBER
The Declaration of Independence and other historic American documents, which had been sent away from Washington for safekeeping in 1941, are put on display at the Library of Congress.

President Roosevelt is elected for a fourth term.

DECEMBER
WRA (Japanese-American internment camps) are ended by federal order.

Popular band leader Glenn Miller dies. He and thousands of other performers traveled to both Europe and the Pacific during the war entertaining troops. Soldier morale is especially boosted by pin up girls like Betty Grable and Jane Russell.

JUNE
U.S. Navy crushes final Japanese naval attack in the Battle of the Philippine Sea.

Powerful B-29 U.S. bombers strike Japan from China, unleashing an air war that will last until summer 1945.

JULY
The capture of Saipan puts Tokyo within range of U.S. B-29 bombers, intensifying the air attacks.

U.S. Marines land on Guam and Tinian.

OCTOBER
The U.S. fleet defeats the Japanese fleet at Leyte Gulf in the largest naval battle in history. Liberation of the Philippines begins.

1945

JANUARY
Nazi death camp at Auschwitz, in Poland, is liberated by the Allies.

Americans defeat the Germans in the Battle of the Bulge.

Soviet troops take control of Poland and march toward Berlin.

FEBRUARY
Churchill, Roosevelt, and Stalin meet in the Soviet city of Yalta to discuss the division of Germany and other postwar issues.

MARCH
U.S. soldiers cross the Rhine River into Germany at Remagen.

U.S. air forces conduct unrelenting bombing attacks against Germany.

U.S. and Soviet forces meet at the Elbe River on the advance to Berlin.

More Nazi death camps are liberated by advancing Allied armies.

Adolf Hitler commits suicide in a Berlin bunker.

MAY
Germany surrenders on May 7 at Eisenhower's headquarters in France.

APRIL
President Roosevelt dies on April 12 during a trip to Warm Springs, Georgia. His Vice President, Harry S. Truman, becomes President.

MAY
Americans celebrate V-E (Victory in Europe) Day on May 8, the day after Germany's surrender.

AUGUST
American celebrate V-J (Victory in Japan) Day on August 15th, the day after Japan's surrender.

JANUARY
U.S. B-29s begin a series of massive firebomb attacks that will cause tremendous damage to Tokyo and other Japanese cities.

MARCH
The most damaging firebomb attack on Tokyo destroys much of the city and wipes out key industrial targets.

AUGUST
A U.S. B-29 flying from Tinian Island drops an atomic bomb on Hiroshima on August 6. Three days later Nagasaki is the target of a second atomic bomb.

Japan's Emperor Hirohito accepts terms of surrender (August 14).

SEPTEMBER 2
Japan signs the surrender documents on the USS *Missouri* in Tokyo Bay.

postscripts: The "kids" who survived and where they are today

EUROPE

Olga Held Bruner married an American G.I. and became one of the first war brides to come to the U.S. She raised a family and then worked as a railroad inspector.

Hedi Wachenheimer worked as an interpreter at the war trials in Nuremberg after the war. When she came to the U.S. in 1948, the immigration officer misspelled her name Hedy. Today, Hedy Epstein lectures nationally and internationally.

Jirina Zizkovska was invited to visit the U.S. as a part of UNICEF in 1948. She was able to stay in the country after President Truman signed a bill for political asylum. She became a citizen in 1955. Currently, she serves as the Czech-Slovak Commissioner on the mayor's Ethnic Enrichment Commission in Kansas City, Missouri.

Fred Losch was a prisoner of war in Russia for two and a half years. After returning to his native Germany he was able to get an American visa. In 1952, he enlisted in the United States Air Force and graduated from college. He served 27 years in the U.S. Air Force before retiring. He lives in the Midwest.

Solange Berger Chomon became a flight attendant for Sabena, Belgium's national airline. On March 11, 2004, she received an award from the President of France for her work in aviation history. She lives with her husband in France.

Libu (Lilly) Lebovitz Segelstein couldn't believe she was going to sleep in a real bed after Auschwitz. She met her future husband in a displaced persons camp in Italy. He had family in New York, so the couple came to the U.S. in 1948, not speaking one word of English. Her husband worked as a tailor and she did piecework as a seamstress.

PACIFIC

Thompson Izawa was a Waikiki lifeguard for 11 years. He received an apology from the U.S. government as a part of the Reparations Act. His hobby is diving for octopus.

Judy Rhoades Davis, along with her mother and sister, left Hawaii on a military convoy ship for the safety of family in Tennessee. She is a retired schoolteacher living in Florida.

Joyce (Joy) Crichton Preston and her family left the Philippines by troopship for California. She became a flight attendant based in the Midwest, where she married and raised a family.

Eiko Arai Moyer found the postwar years as hard as the war years. She married an American G.I. and lives in Independence, Missouri, President Truman's hometown, where she is a dress designer.

HOME FRONT

James J. Fisher is a retired prize-winning newspaper reporter living in the Midwest.

Allan Hida and his family moved to Wisconsin upon their release from Amache Camp. He is retired after teaching for 30 years. He frequently gives talks about his internment camp experiences.

Dora Mae Boone Traul and Betty Jo Oetting Morris stayed in the Midwest, where they married and raised their families.

Dorinda Makanaōnalani Stagner lived in Pearl City Peninsula, until her junior year of high school when the Navy forced all civilians to leave. She won a hula contest, which brought her to the mainland United States. She became a flight attendant and married Larry Nicholson. She is now an author and psychotherapist, living in Raytown, Missouri.

Rubber for tires and gasoline was so scarce during the war that the speed limit was reduced to 35 miles per hour.

bibliography

Ambrose, Stephen. *The Good Fight: How World War II Was Won.* New York: Atheneum Books for Young Readers, 2001.

Anderson, C. LeRoy, Joanne R. Anderson, Yunoshuke Ohkura, editors. *No Longer Silent: World-wide Memories of the Children of World War II.* Missoula, MT: Pictorial Histories Publishing, 1995.

Andrews, Harris, John Bolster, Steve Hyslop, and Jim Lynch. *An Illustrated History of World War II, Crisis & Courage: Humanity on the Brink.* New York: Time-Life Books, 2001.

Bruner, Olga Held. *A German War Bride's Story.* Olathe, KS: PLB Publishing, 2000.

Churchill, Winston. *The Second World War Illustrated & Abridged.* Surrey, United Kingdom: TAJ Books, 2003.

Cooper, Michael. *Fighting for Honor: Japanese Americans and World War II.* New York: Clarion Books, 2000.

Losch, Fred. *Opa's Tales: An Odyssey from War Torn East Prussia to the American Midwest.* New York: Writers Club Press, 2002.

Nicholson, Dorinda M. *Pearl Harbor Child.* Honolulu, Hawaii: Arizona Memorial Association, 1993.

Panchyk, Richard. *World War II for Kids.* Chicago: Chicago Review Press, Inc., 2002.

Werner, Emmy. *Through the Eyes of Innocents: Children Witness World War II.* Boulder, CO: Westview Press, 2000.

index

educational extensions

1. What is the "foreword" of a book? How does a book's foreword add meaning to the text? Read the foreword of *Remember World War II* and research its author, Madeleine K. Albright. Why do you think she was chosen to write the foreword? What important background information did you gain about the topic?

2. How does the structure of the text contribute to its effectiveness? Describe the structure of *Remember World War II*. Give examples of how the presentation of information, including sidebars, photography, and additional information, added to your understanding of the content.

3. How does an individual's personal experience enhance our understanding of history? Choose three personal accounts from the text and compare different perspectives on the war. Distinguish between fact, opinion, and reasoned judgment. Analyze the relationship between primary and secondary sources.

4. Discuss what Nicholson means by "If we want lasting peace, we would do well to look to the children of war in every generation" (page 57). How can this concept be applied to your life or the world around you?

more to ponder ...

- Why do authors write nonfiction? How can reading nonfiction shape our ideas, values, beliefs, and behaviors?

- What can we learn from reading real-life accounts of history? How are you affected when reading different points of view? How do the histories of earlier groups and individuals influence later generations?

- How has the world changed from the time period of the text? How do you think it will change in the future?

- Research a topic from the book. Compare and contrast information and details that you found from different sources.